MW00531835

Also by Spencer Reece

POETRY

The Road to Emmaus
The Clerk's Tale

PROSE

The Secret Gospel of Mark: A Poet's Memoir

AS EDITOR

Counting Time Like People Count Stars: Poems by
the Girls of Our Little Roses, San Pedro Sula, Honduras

WATERCOLORS

All the Beauty Still Left: A Poet's Painted Book of Hours

ACTS

SPENCER

ACTS POEMS

REECE

FARRAR

STRAUS

GIROUX

NEW

YORK

Farrar, Straus and Giroux
120 Broadway, New York 10271

Copyright © 2024 by Spencer Reece
All rights reserved
Printed in the United States of America
First edition, 2024

Grateful acknowledgment is made for permission to reprint the
following previously published and unpublished material: Lines from
"De pronto," by Francisco García Lorca, reprinted by permission of
the Estate of Francisco García Lorca. Lines from "The Mower," from
The Complete Poems of Philip Larkin, by Philip Larkin, edited by Archie
Burnett. Copyright © 2012 by the Estate of Philip Larkin. Reprinted
by permission of Farrar, Straus and Giroux and Faber and Faber, Ltd. All
rights reserved. "Peregrino," from the book *Desolación de la Quimera, 1956–1962*
(Part XI of *La Realidad y el Deseo*), by Luis Cernuda. Copyright © the Estate
of Luis Cernuda. Excerpt from *Amor de Don Perlimplín con Belisa en su jardín*, by
Federico García Lorca, copyright © Herederos de Federico García Lorca.
Reprinted by permission of the Estate of Federico García Lorca.

Illustration on pages ii and 103 courtesy of the author.

Library of Congress Cataloging-in-Publication Data
Names: Reece, Spencer, author.
Title: Acts : poems / Spencer Reece.
Description: First edition. | New York : Farrar, Straus and Giroux, 2024.
Identifiers: LCCN 2023050745 | ISBN 9780374100834 (hardback)
Subjects: LCGFT: Poetry.
Classification: LCC PS3618.E4354 A64 2024 | DDC 811/.6—dc23/eng/20231127
LC record available at https://lccn.loc.gov/2023050745

Designed by Crisis

Our books may be purchased in bulk for promotional,
educational, or business use. Please contact your local bookseller
or the Macmillan Corporate and Premium Sales Department
at 1-800-221-7945, extension 5442, or by email at
MacmillanSpecialMarkets@macmillan.com.

www.fsgbooks.com
Follow us on social media at @fsgbooks

1 3 5 7 9 10 8 6 4 2

The thing that is important to know is that you never know.

——DIANE ARBUS

CONTENTS

ACTS

SAN SEBASTIÁN

¡Ay, ay, ay!

Still singing in my cell.
Nothing personal. Never was.
How often I get that wrong . . .
Some man is always fleeing,
and that is never personal.

Longer I go fewer notes
I need. *Give me your hand, love,*
once more, so this fatal wound
will do its work.
My torso swells—
a hotel. *The deep wound of love*
flown—Martyrdom bores me.
My hookup my flamenco—

Will I be saved?

Yes, Goddammit,
I will be saved. Pitch your vile tracts.
Peninsula, tilt your goblets.
I measure God through my acts.

Pierced, cherished, penned—
I am alone.
                    Wasn't I always?
Wasn't I?

    Swifts fleck the dry grass.
O this wound!

    By my absence you'll know me.

SANCTUS

A cathedral
without
a bell

a mouth
without
a tongue

a pillaged
pyramid
in Madrid

between
services
the Bishop

purple shirt
white ruffles
gold cope

chasuble
a mitre
lappets

a firefighter
decorated
with his rig

he sweats
he spins
the tin

globe
unoiled
for years

screeching
like a massacre
crisscrossed

with lines
charting
Columbus

O Israel
help me
arise

recount
recalibrate
save

dispatch
a story
of tenderness

LA SANTA CENA

FOR REVEREND SCOTT WALTERS

Roving gold Segovia
your Roman aqueduct
your closed museum
Machado's piss pot
tan fields of wheat

the large buses chuff
doors always locked
we are five no four
stuck in a storefront
a stained rained-on page

taped to the tinted glass
lists our hour wrong
once a month
I say mass
hold my box that snaps

soiled by the palms
of our priest shot dead
under that squat fat

teeny-weeny dictator
corrugated nicked cover

inside the host molds
the wine turpentine
they don't listen much
my accent is off
more of a loud cough

broken up by a lisp
I measure our savior
Todo está preparado
Acercaos a la mesa de Dios
it's over quick

they feed me
tortilla de patatas Coke
and tarta de Santiago
this gruff yellow land
drenched in manure

Plath hated Spain
she was young
Ted hadn't left yet
this republic requires
respect age inures

the large sky like foil
crackles in the olive grove
I lay my old head
on the foldout bed
where a mattress coil

pokes my backbone
Oh, to be loved like this

IN SOLITARIA STANZA

He will paint his mother
with shades of burgundy,
the color watered down,
and a mint green accent.

At the end of the end
of the end of a cul-de-sac,
she sits parsing her life
out like a set of pills:

"Darling, once we went
to Chartwell and saw
where Churchill painted."
He strives to be clear.

He always paints what
isn't there, but *is* there,
much like her dementia.
Would it be fair to say—

all art wants the truth?
The aide talks baby talk:
"Time to wash you up!"
January. Connecticut.

I have yet many things
to say unto you but ye
cannot bear them now.
Inconsequential pair,

the estates with fences
take little note of them.
Her wheelchair shines—
Blake's chariot of fire.

O dumb twee colosseum
of busted thingamabobs,
wandering Jew cuttings,
illegible sticky-notes!

He mixes Payne's gray
for the living room walls.
Fills in the bookcase—
staccato russet brown dabs.

Wipes her red bottom.
Cuts up her skirt steak.
She weeps. She yells.
Painting is the kinder art.

LETTERS FROM SPAIN

FOR ERIC FRIESEN

En el país de los ciegos, el tuerto es rey.
—Spanish proverb

Mis primeros días aquí en Madrid

I don't want to make mistakes—but Lord
I make them, didn't wear the right shoes
(black running shoes instead of dress shoes),
answered the phone wrong, welcomed wrong,
was told never to wear gloves in the church
even though we have no heat.
                          My Spanish
is delicate—I misunderstand each liturgy:
I bow when we stand, I kneel when we sit, I sing
when we pray. This is not the Episcopal church
as I know it: not one Lilly Pulitzer shift in sight.
This phrase I recite: ¡Os pido que tengáis
paciencia con mi castellano! Often
my Spanish syllables bumble out my lips
and test the patience of the faithful in the front.
I'm fairly sure no one is listening.

All my priest shirts bloom with sweat stains.
Word reached me from Christ Church, Westerly!
Natalie Lawton fills me in with each letter
she writes. Fall now.

 The ordination went well, although
hardly anyone came! A bicycle race cut off access
with its thousands of wheels—
it was my parents' last plane flight.
We were surrounded by muscles in spandex.
The erotic barely contained: that was a sign.
When I landed Aloysi Busquets collected me.
His first name pronounced Al-oh-we-see.
He talks quick. His story I can't track.
Poor, imprisoned, a soldier, a welder, he left
a wife and child in Cuba, but why I'm not sure.
He uses the word vergüenza. Need to look that up.
In Cuba injustice was done to him. He told me
Catholic priests have sex. At least I think
that's what he said.

Algunas semanas después

The Bishop and I translated a letter
about Saint Willibrord for the Old Catholics,
a saint who evangelized with questionable success
and knew discord. El Obispo's paunch leans on me,
warms me as a hen warms an egg.

Aloysi speaks confidently of eternity,
he takes a microphone and drum machine
to the Metro, where he seeks to convert.
He loves a woman in the church—spaces
between his teeth—he said to me last week,
"Top Secret." His joy pleases me. Faces with joy
please me, know what I mean? Down the street
Belarusian prostitutes anoint men with spit.
Who isn't on their knees begging please?
Who isn't groomed by the tyranny of an hour?

Every morning I drink my strong coffee
and look at this photo I framed of Natalie Lawton.
In it, she's just about to put the red stole
on me for my deaconate ordination.

I linger in front of her as with a relic.
Before I enter the cathedral, I dust her off.
Madrid is dusty.

How did her last note begin?

"You have no idea how much your letters
cheer me up! I am alone a lot . . . ," Natalie wrote
in a cursive no longer taught.

Much has gone:
The Palacio de Cibeles, our grand post office,
is now a museum. The letter slots sealed.
No one goes there. The pen's throat is sore.
Auden hated the typewriter: he believed
that clatter of keys ruined his poems.
He had no idea what lay ahead. Thank God
I have the letters Natalie wrote—

Natalie in your pew, second on the right,
your fine white hair permed like a lamb's coat . . .

Cotidiano

The jet lag was bad! You go and go
against time. When I first arrived, I hugged
El Obispo! A big American hug. He told me Spaniards
do *not* hug when they first meet. Awkward—
as you might imagine. Many things the Bishop
attributes to Spaniards I find belong solely to him.
Still. My ways stand out. Well, I am what I am . . .
"and have not been called in vain . . ."—isn't that
what Paul says somewhere? Saturday now.
Aloysi and I must collect food in our old van
called a furgoneta. I'll read the Bible in Castilian
and he'll correct me.

El Obispo picks at the hair in his ears—
last of his plumage.

Today I recall how Natalie made me feel . . .
At the Shelter Harbor Inn she used her gift certificate.
Her son washed dishes in the back. She told me
she believed in me. Few talk like that.
Last thing Natalie asked about was my work.

I'm the Bishop's secretario, a keeper of secrets,
before me six or seven former ones came to bad
or mysterious ends like Henry the Eighth's wives.
They are mentioned in hushed tones.
I shuffle papers, check email, write letters
(we still do), keep track of Ordinary Time,
always shifting, recall appointments
(never on time), answer the door, which gets stuck,
celebrate the mass, attendance sparse, Spaniards
prefer movies, open and close the door for AA,
dust off all the Bishop's whatchamajiggers,
recount and recount all the offering figures,
put the rent in hiding places, and on the dirty rag rug
I use the broken taped vacuum that fails to suck.

Navidad

It's cold! I write with my coat on
and there's no hot water in the sink. No snow.
Hasn't snowed for years. When it does it sticks
to the statue of the Devil as a fallen angel. Spaniards
claim this is the *only* statue of the Devil—
not true, but Spaniards say so.

                        This city where poetry died.
While Franco closed our cathedral, Machado
and his mother died on a march. She watched her son
die first. He had a poem in his pocket. Hernández
died in prison. His eyes remained open. Cernuda
left. Behind him a girl's legs got blown off.
Lorca they killed because he was a maricón.

Aloysi punched the anarchist atheist
who sassed back—Mucho ruido, pocas nueces,
Aloito said. You know the one—big cysts—
the one who carts off rotten quinces in crates.
I laughed. El Obispo said it was *not* funny:
priests shouldn't punch anyone in the face.

All at once this country lost its voice.
Our cathedral shuttered for forty years. Christmas
soon. I spread the faith best I can, in my ways,
but it's slow, slow, slow. Not having toilet paper for guests
doesn't help, the faithful filch what they can.
Vipers who walk off with the donated diapers.
Maligned, odd, microscopic bishopric!
When I call British priests they don't pick up.
Our "close" consists of rancid garbage and behind it,
old married gays in open relationships.
My three rooms—since you ask—are at the top;
if you climb the stairs the honeyed wood
will creak like organ pedals. There's a locked library
with names I can't recall: Athanasius,
Apollinaris of *something*, the Montanists—
laughed at like us.

                        I clean the place when I can.

Reyes

When Spaniards speak fast I'm lost.
They call me a silly American when they think
I can't hear. I send postcards to old girlfriends
and hesitate to say it but I'm fairly sure
I found a man named Manuel on an app.
Nearly all men there were named Manuel.
Adam4Adam, Silverdaddies, or Gaydar,
I'll try not to sound sure about what's unsure.
He's muscular. Hardly speaks English.
Selfishness is love's cousin, said Keats.
Best I return to my task of relabeling labels
with the names of our far-flung priests.

Something sings through the mildew.
Is it El Obispo, who has a fish and three small birds?
Every morning now he tenderly addresses them
among the plants he has planted in rusted oil drums.
Often the birds get stolen. He looks sad then.
Only I see this. Maybe his elegant wife sees it.
We rarely see her, she's busy. And more beautiful
than us. They have no children, only two Yorkies

named Honey and Sugar: a kind of future.
They wiggle in the sacristy like go-go dancers.
Spaniards whisper as if nothing had less hope
than to be childless and worship without the Pope.
Once the Bishop cried but I don't speak of this.

On Calle Amor de Dios, old ladies in lipstick
and fur coats smoke and come up to my hips.
Last year I went to Memphis, saw Scott and Ardelle,
stood before the Lorraine Motel, where America
died some.

Out the window now: this city of dead Empire.

Cuaresma

Our plastic priest collars, tossed off,
resemble nail crescents clipped from big toes.
Why does my Bishop trust me so?
How can I understand being born into a dictatorship?
Being elected young for a church about to fall apart?
Having all your property confiscated?
Knowing people who died for their faith?
What do I know?

El Obispo named his turtle Tortuga.
An austere choice but the Bishop *is* austere:
He wears old stained trousers and lives in the dark
to save on electric. Tortuga begins to search—
he wants touch the way we all want touch.
Who knows his age or sex?
                              The Bishop in a cape
enters the office to light wax pots with a flourish.
We time when to press his ring on the wax.
Then I send letters to the Archbishop, His Grace,
but I'm fairly sure they get misplaced. I possess
a peculiar dumb and unidentified loneliness.
In the front door, a peephole to view guests.
A Brit knocked and was ignored.

Elizabeth O'Reilly in the 1800s
was a missionary to Spain. When she came home
her sister committed her to a mental hospital.
A cautionary tale.

My Bishop chortles. It's not
dull. I am the matador, he the bull.
Every day Señor Gómez visits. Retired, mysterious,
four feet tall with his leather fedora, he sits
mute in my office for hours. Once he showed us
a picture from the 1940s, and *there he was*
with the *same* fedora! I move around him.
He might have been harmed under Franco.

Maybe he's gay, someone once said so.
Hard to tell, though, and who's to say?

Pascua

My sink is a set of unworkable hoses.
The Bishop says it will be fixed; so I wait
as the Israelites did with Moses. A chandelier sits
on the floor for decades. Sometimes a chair,
broken, finds a use like the resting spot
for Señor Gómez. Waiting is the cathedral's spell.

On Facebook a second cousin posts:
Huntsville, Alabama—single mom, son biracial,
almost twelve, *Our next Barack! Here he is
in a baseball uniform, ready to swing his bat.*
Likes. Hearts. Emojis. GIFs. Last kin I've got.
No letters between us as of yet.

My Bishop said we must consecrate
a former peluquería, where once men tended
one another, like the moon to the sea, now
we will offer the host with bad lighting.

Someone stole our car radio.
El Obispo sang hymns for over an hour,

scenery blurred, his voice off-key. I listened
in the little car. He failed to recall the tune and words—
he sang in many high-pitched strong blanks—
excruciating, yet plaintive. Finally, we arrived
at our new church plant, a basement strip club
in Navalcarnero. I carried his mitre and cope
in the shopping bag. His staff unfolds like those sticks
for the blind. When done, we zoomed past
olive groves and trashed movie houses hollow
as the church. In the car the Bishop tells me never
to fret. He is kind, which differs from nice.
Sometimes with me he invents words like
"Don't be preoccupated."

Fiesta de los Mártires de la Reforma Española

You asked about the cathedral—
it began late after the Inquisition ended.
One last Anglican was burned and then
Archbishop Plunkett from Dublin gave the funds
(the Irish knew slights). But just as we got going
Franco came, he who harpooned whales from his yacht.
El Obispo shakes his head, things painful to say—
our priests shot in the head. Franco hated
the Protestant. An "extra-provincial jurisdiction"—
Britain and the States send no money unless I ask.
So it goes, no money no memory, no memory no money.
So I ask and ask and ask and routinely I hear:
"We have a cathedral there?"

My Bishop is bald, *even* the sides thin,
strands stipple the scalp. Last year the Bishop
lost the sight in one eye, a stroke. We are both
in our midfifties and sigh over age's advance.
I speak to the good eye while the other floats. I lean
over him each day and place three sets of drops
into the jelly of the bad eye, often infected—

pus collects in the socket. Doctors debate
whether to cut it out. I rotate around
the glaucous unworkable dead orb like a clock,
keeping his many confidences. He's put on weight,
has gout. Yesterday, his cassock seam ripped.
The rip quacked like a duck—then we prayed.
Next week he'll have six teeth pulled.
He spoke of San Isidro, Spain's saint who took a siesta
while the angels did all his work. Explains much.

Word came Natalie Lawton died—
fell outside CVS. I wept.

Pentecostés

¿Por qué estáis mirando al cielo?
—Hechos 1:11

A few months back we went down to Huelva
to clean our graveyard—condoms hung
from the saplings shooting up from the dead:
British fighter pilots mainly, and an American.
My Bishop chainsawed brush and got welts
from the sap. I followed with a wheelbarrow.
Dressed in my clericals.
                              Townsfolk laughed.
I think about my country and hope this reaches you—
as Lorca hoped his poems might reach us.
I think of Natalie's son washing plates in the back.
I see those New Englanders brush crumbs away.
Sometimes I feel out of place but then I think
of Katharine Lee Bates, who wrote our famous hymn,
was a missionary to Spain, a discreet lesbian.

Viggo Mortensen was in our post office.
Viggo's older, adjusting to not being seen.

29

What comes after that?

Spain seems kinder.

Natalie Lawton, the last of the letter writers,
is gone. I think of Natalie now with the Holy Spirit.
We used to say Holy Ghost but now we don't—
our British organist with hemorrhoids,
one of the only Anglican things we've got,
sitting on her foam donut
said the church thought it too Halloween.

Upstairs the chandelier sparkles on the floor
and the instructions for heat are painted over—
they look like Braille.

Wait. Someone's at the door.

Fiesta de Corpus Christi

Peter is no longer with us. Did I tell you?
Did I mention him? Guileless fellow.
Forgot his last name. Began with a "c"?
Late seventies, reticent, sang in the choir,
muttered, carried no note, served on no committee,
never put cash in the offering.
Said we stole his money until we realized
Aloysi's stepson was a kleptomaniac.

Somehow, he became my ad hoc charge.
Married twice, the exes I couldn't reach.
No children. Left messages, sent emails
to family members back in Harrogate.
A bartender said, "Peter came to Madrid
for Corpus Christi in 1970 and never left."
Madrid!

Madrid beds you right after "¿Como estás?"
and never relents. Peter lived with us in a room
with leaks. No heat. His things in one suitcase.
From his cot he strummed flamenco on a guitar

with one string, then the music stopped.
He was in the Navy, taught kids English.
"Nothing significant," he said. Before I knew it,
I was cutting his toenails, washing him up
as he talked about what he did for old Blighty—
love between men: Huck Finn and Jim,
Lincoln and Speed.

     Yesterday he fell down the Metro stairs.
The police sent him away in restraints.
A British priest said, "Send him to the Queen.
Best he be now with his own." But, but—
once you're gone do you exist? I can still smell
Peter on the stairs, it's almost bearable.
Whatever the question the answer is love.
He's in one of those tercera edad places.
Card games, bleach. I forget the address.
It's late. The night grows sexy and tall.
Time to lock the cathedral. Hope I see you
before too long.
               Abrazos desde Madrid—

El año siguiente

I thought I'd be in Madrid one year.
Then the Bishop asked *me back.* When I left
he actually hugged *me.* Let that be noted please.
I'd thought the whole thing was temporary
but then much is temporary, or so it feels.
The work found me and so it is right. The Bishop
and his wife got another Yorkie, named it Candy.
Manuel dumped me. Miss our walks under trees,
his biceps big piglets, our striptease, and more—
what? The way he moved, that strut—his flamenco.
But he was not out.

A missionary here disapproves of the gays
(even though his son is one), he told me he pays
to get *it* undone. Much goes unspoken,
between the cracks when the bread is broken
in a city thick and passive with Catholics.
Biblical texts that discount sex are of no use
in a city that excels at the art of the guess.
The wives of the missionaries all have IBS,
long nights they lie on squeaky cots and twitch
and twist—their intestines knotted from stress.

    Yesterday I thought of Amy Lowell
here on my street called Calle de la Beneficencia
(odd cognate beneficence, almost, well, *Episcopal*).
Lowell's poems rarely get heard: what we recall
is her will, responsible for bringing poets everywhere.
Mysterious art where little is custodial.
I'm far from home.

    Love, love. Love is best when not my idea.

Muchos años después

   They buried Natalie Lawton in Rhode Island.
Is that the smallest state or is it Delaware?
As my dead mount and I read Ecclesiastes
drone on about how the dead are not handy,
I disagree. Legions have left their mark on me.
I think to write a long letter to Donald Hall,
the last poet to write me letters—but then I forget
or emails overtake the screen.

   During the Guerra Civil, three priests
were shot—*Pow! Pow! Pow!*—
from this church by Franco's firing squads,
their bodies never recovered.
Once they paced and stood where I now labor.

   Letters started in the Book of Acts.
Luke wrote to Theophilus in his dusty office,
much like mine, about how the spirit shook
from Cephas to the twelve to the five hundred.
Acts is the biography of the Holy Spirit,
tracking the story of how the faith spread
with bread and spit and letters.

Yesterday in AA a man joked about gays,
mocked the way feminine men walk, talk.
I stopped the meeting. Shut the instigator up
like Jesus in Dostoevsky, no people-pleaser he.
So it goes in our rinky-dink cockamamie see,
our mattresses stained with life's discharge,
and out cracked windows, tourists with selfie-sticks
swarm around our ruin held together by grants
I weasel out of Trinity Wall Street.
"Poorest diocese in the Communion,"
said an old priest picking his nose
patched with a bad skin graft. Back I trudged
to our bus station of an office. Made no mention
of what I'd done. Sat with my Bishop
under our broken clock. God, I loved him
and thought to tell him so
                              but I did not.

Ayer

The other day the Bishop yelled at me,
I can't say berating me was his goal, but—
we were in the back courtyard, by the cross
made from toilet tubes, shaded by the avocado tree.
I had finished preaching my homilía:
Los diez leprosos son sanados por el Espíritu Santo.
Only *one* leper says thanks. If Jesus thought
he was going to be adored he was mistaken.
Love is an invisible business.
I mentioned grace at the eleven o'clock:
El Espíritu Santo no elige favoritos,
la gracia recae sobre las personas
que son agradecidas y las que son ingratas.

I made ten visits to my window at nightfall.
Taxis orbited the Plaza de Colón. After our spat,
the Bishop knocked, produced a pup,
a small black and white hum and squeak.
He had spent the day visiting churches
and a gypsy who was begging for the host,
crossing a country once divided the way mine

had been by Robert E. Lee and the Confederacy.
Along the way he found an abandoned moist
motherless mongrel that mewled, and I mean
mewled. The nameless carefree thing
squirmed with the extravagance of health.

"Para tí," El Obispo said. "He's andaluz."
Well, what could I do? I forgave the Bishop again.
A Spanish smile spread across his cheeks
like a flag, and perhaps he forgave me too:
can't be sure. God knows I wasn't always easy.
El Obispo says: "I know I'm difficult, don't say
I'm not." Our faces fix like the long-married.
Forgiveness: our most rewarding emotion.

Hoy

Outside our dusty iron window bars,
Madrid's largest gay gym. A muscular man exits
with a French bulldog who shakes his buttocks
like maracas and tugs his owner, who unfurls
a plastic bag to scoop up his shits.

                                        I tilt toward
the emails—the screen warms me. I look like
I am too close to a painting at the Prado—
Rembrandt's self-portrait as crusty Paul.
My cheek warms as the earth does with the sun.
I smell of a peeled orange and a salchichón fart.
I count all the coins in plastic bags—
the treasuries for the twelve-step groups.

Our weekly church newsletter is called *La Hoja*.
I've done *La Hoja* with errors (again!):
wrong texts, misspelled names, misidentified pictures.
Then printed one hundred copies and sent it out
through the entire country of Spain and beyond.
El Obispo fumes: "I can't believe you are so stupid!
You walk around here with your head in the clouds!"

Then he mumbles something harsh, a Spanish dicho
about crabs stuck in a bucket. "Americans!"
he huffs. "They can't handle me, apart from you."

 Once I forgot everything and stalled at the altar
like the halt in the gospels: guess who bolted
from the sacristy, steadied me, and held my hand?
I use Don with El Obispo like Quixote.
Never once his naked Christian name.
Lambeth Palace denied us the grant.
My Spanish Protestant looks small then, but noble.
In London the Archbishop sneered and I failed
to translate the nuances into Spanish.
On our single hard English mattresses,
we prayed.
 The word hope comes from bent;
when I think of El Obispo I know what they meant.

Mi último día aquí

I hate the apartment packed.
I write this among bare walls, mildew stains,
and nail holes. I grow obsolete among the blue tiles.
The vet gave me a pill to knock out the pup.
I gave away what I could. I said goodbye
to the bookstore, Desperate Literature,
named after something Bolaño wrote,
walked the streets of Chueca one last time,
pondered Manuel—"Gracias, mi amor."
I assume he forgot me or needed to forget me—
love can grow with forgetfulness.

Paul saw faith in Timothy as if faith
were a gene. Perhaps. All of us descended
from that pretty boy nailed to a tree.
Maybe some of El Obispo will be in me?
What happens now?

I leave Luis Muñoz writing poems
in the city where lovers die and poetry lives.
I bid goodbye to Plaza Santa Ana,

where Hemingway drank, I stand before
the statue of Lorca with his pájaro.
As El Obispo once more fingers the thin pages
of our broken, taped Bible like cash
I think to tell him, "Federico
fué el primer secretario para toda España!"
But I have run out of time for caprice.

   Lorca said to me: "Pero ¿por qué? ¿por qué
me atormentas? ¿Cómo no vienes conmigo,
si me amas, hasta dónde yo te lleve?"

   In Jackson Heights, Queens—
Padre Antonio from the República Dominicana
has died of Covid—Would I consider?

   Orphan of Spain, where will I go?

La madrugada después de mi salida

Plaza Santa María, church bells ring—
the ax of the Holy Spirit. Catholic bells, no bells
for Protestants. The fluorescent light shut off
in the smelly office for the most unknown cathedral
on the globe. Under the stars Madrid glows,
the chandelier of Europe lit with empty churches.
I will never love a city more than this one.
Every night love disrobes on nonsensical streets.

Up, up, up above, planets bob on their strings,
part of some implausible mobile, suspending us
in infinity where angels and archangels wander.
But who made the strings? What lies beyond?
Is there a wall? Or no wall at all? Up there?
Just universe after universe after universe?
I know, I know, impossible to ponder too long.

The Bishop of Spain lurches to the front door,
a mother bear, dragging his minuscule suitcase
behind him, the size of a wastepaper basket.
I know he wears his giant silver cross around his neck

that swings like a great clapper in a bell.
I know he holds his man-purse, referred to between us
as his little fag bag, in Spanish a mariconera.
I know he clutches a black fan called an abanico.
I know he readjusts his bishop ring on his left hand.
I know he will turn to the right.
                                        The speed train
will get him to Santiago by six in the morning.
His iPhone will ping-ping as nuance is thrust upon him,
a windfall of late middle age. O El Obispo! El Obispo!
Once at a giant church thing in the States,
priests slurping Starbucks on a hard ugly busy rug,
my knees throbbed and our work was mocked:
Was it true I worked all those years without a pension?

    Faith, faith, Tomás Morín, since you asked,
settles on Madrid, an afterthought, the thing
that happens *after* thought and what happens
after that.

Mañana por la mañana

Clouds advance in their armada—
I'm headed home, wherever that might be.
Home, what word warms the tongue more?
In my tight seat, we fly toward JFK.
George Herbert on my tray, the dog, drugged
under the seat in front of me. —And church?
On Calle de la Beneficencia? You will go on
and be late, late, late, very late—

Aloysi! Flip the circuit breakers!
Click, click, click, ilumina la catedral!
Bag the grub: fruits, tubers, spuds, the beet,
its ruby religion: ¡Cógelo y ven acá!
Light up the biblical saying on the wall:
Sacrifica a Dios alabanza, y paga tus votos
al Altísimo. The heat will not work.
No me digas. The Metro will rumble.
People will line up for their bags of food;
some will pray, others will shout into cell phones,
waiting for handouts. Two old ladies
will sit and chitchat about God. Go on! Go on!
Go on!

Will take years, but eventually
a new cleric will arrive and replace me,
and hold out the money plate. Hazlo! Hazlo!
And here's a tambourine, a pandereta
while you're at it . . . And who knows?
"La puerta está abierta siempre, Espencer,"
El Obispo said. O Spanish slowness,
generous, graceful, meticulous, kind—
Thornton Wilder once said it takes a year
to get a letter from Spain. España, España,
te quiero muchísimo, no encuentro
las palabras para expresarlo.

Predica, Aloysi, predica!

Sing, Bishop, sing!

TRES CREPÚSCULOS

I take my journey into Spain.
—Romans 15:24

Uno

Let the itchy peninsula's gored bulls
bleed let her trains with rapacious tourists speed
to Aranjuez let her ignored Africans lay out
faux-Gucci sunglasses and knockoff doohickeys
on white tarmacs let the scared scarred men scoop
up their stuff in sacks and scatter when police lurk

Rubén Rubén Rubén above me Christ
sags in his candelabra of surrender sending up
flares old women tut-tut and hold tissues cemented
with snot and tend his plaster of Paris nudity
delivering onto them his news of how we touch
and are speckled with slivers of the moon
how we shine in the night like wedding silver
muscle on muscle let us follow him like runts
I qualify before the old-timers to say poetry
is close to outer space and this this is where
we will be so happy for a time yes indeed Manuel
Rafa Abio our gristle sparkles and stars spill
their milk as salty beds swallow us

poetry is what we do while we wait
to come into the kingdom where what we see
is not how it went poetry is all of Portugal
Pessoa kept populating my Bible is a rag to sop
up messes the evening fills with condoms videos
and slop and the slick devotion of sex for sex's sake
the moon licks Madrid's razor-shaved freckled neck
the Spanish stars French-kiss everyone so that
they surround us as the British did before
Admiral Federico Gravina at the Battle of Trafalgar
who lost an arm as yellow fever raged Rubén the love
with which the stars love us is in us and we
are in them I swear to you I swear I swear
by all the sugar blood and sap of the animals
I swear there is not one thing in this universe
no not one thing nor the universe beyond full of holes
and planets and asteroids that is not buried
with opportunity and desire

Dos

Now it was said to me *Silly man*
do you think there isn't one person in la catedral
who doesn't know what you are with that voice
of yours? That swish? Kind brutal Spanish
go my days mi hermano dubbed flubbed snubbed
evening charges and licks Madrid the rose light
stains us with radical surrender that Christ
loved Rubén now listen even my own Goddamned mother
knew what it was I was or thought I was whatever
it was I was for Christ's sake so what's the problem

when Spaniards conquered the Apache
they cut off the right foot of every young man
over the age of twenty-five and watched them
hop about the dirt on their squirting stumps
cruelty shouldn't surprise but oh it does it does
this is where poetry can be of some use no
for poetry is the opposite of cruelty poetry O poetry

guapetones oil their fluted biceps
expanding in bedrooms dry as crypts thrumming

on all fours someone dominates beneath Christ
Padre Hijo y Espíritu Santo say we mammals
nipples alert as doorbells ringing who among us
does not crave breasts O fecund rotundas
over our sharp hearts Alaska sings
¿A quién le importa lo que yo diga?
Yo soy así, y así seguiré, ¡nunca cambiaré!
there's a piss-soaked nook at the corner
of Hortaleza and Augusto Figueroa littered
with cigarette butts Rubén Quesada
a bowlegged Russian escort swaggers
with pockets full of euros in Chueca that smells
of leftover jizz-rags from Skype-sex filling
damp hampers O my musculitos the day fires
endowed with the nectar of suitors Rubén Quesada
chaperoned by the moon's one exhausted eyeball
boring a hole into the back of my skull like grapeshot
I surrender I surrender I surrender I surrender

Tres

　　Rubén Quesada young poet
remember whatever happens I love you
poetry is radical love radical for this reason
poetry is next to Christ poetry has a frayed cord
with a plug that shorts and a bulb that flickers
out the broken window covered with a fine film
of dust poetry is an old pug upstaging the universe
poetry is this pathetic river trickling through Madrid
singing an itsy-bitsy ditty to the shivering drunks
what's that river called

　　snagging the failing light as on the back
of a black snake the river is poetry poetry is the river
we disperse into the parched gelatinous night
where the horny Panero family once roamed
honoring their country with poems poems
devoting their groins to extinction like monks

　　I examine postulants who are sinking
like a fleet for el orden sagrado del presbiterado
asking the newly pious about Christ's stinking feet

his continuous two-thousand-year-old funeral
many are righteous too righteous pity the righteous
the righteous have not surrendered Rubén and P.S.
righteousness bores the bejesus out of the universe
can you see now the cornices and setbacks
of the Telefónica Building shine they have turned
to the color of God and the windows are cold
as distant planets where Hemingway sent out
his reports before bedding Martha Gellhorn
Rubén Quesada Rubén Quesada sex is
complicated sex is not complicated sex is
sex men and women sext laying down dirty words
and nude shots in a greased trail their thumbs
like snails unshaved Madrid doused in piss
the old Spanish moon falls like an ax
on my cracked desk as I glue tiny pieces
of my laughed-at religion back together again

SPANISH DANCES

FOR HUGH HAUGHTON & KIT FAN

But the most indelible event that etched itself on the tablets of the memory of Juan was the death of the great Spanish poet Antonio Machado, who had crossed the border in their company. "It was as though Spain itself were dying," he said.
—Philip Levine, "Living in Machado"

1.

Spain, you smell like cigarettes—
generous, plump, never grumpy about sex,
when in repose you growl and snap
about your short girlie-voiced dictator.

Gitanos scatter under the archways,
shoulders like shovels, they maraud
and mooch with rosemary sprigs.
My scarf flows from my throat.

I lug my truth around the world.
Old American, boina over my thin hair.
I am responsible to a gassy rescue pup
who gloms on to me like an escort.

In Granada, a blind woman befriends me.
Her eyeballs roll back like coffee cups.
She teaches me dirty words in the park—
like caraculo which means ass-face.

She says one of Lorca's close friends
died at the hands of Franco's troops—
they crushed his glasses into his face,
he bled through his eye sockets.

El crimen fue en Granada . . .
Machado whispers as Spaniards ready
for siestas, kick off shoes, unbuckle belts.
A used condom blows into Lorca's ditch.

2.

Caminante, I want nothing but my mutt pup—
magnanimous as a Velázquez court dwarf.
The moon spreads across the pueblo
like a crisis and I have my worries

which add nothing. Nothing! Palacio,
buen amigo, Europe is in crisis.
In these years the Lorca sisters cry.
The rumor goes round they've found

Federico's corpse. Is it a hoax?
Machado marched until he died . . .
Tonight rain leaks into the wall
filling my eardrums with its riot.

I think the rain is Machado
come to tell me to be quiet, very quiet . . .
Enriqueta Carbonell wrote a note.
I am so very sorry to bother you with this . . .

She had two small girls. They shot
her husband. We can't find his body.

Unamuno, sometimes at night I see
those Jewish liberal boys from Brooklyn

who got their heads blown off.
The Republicans had no helmets.
They wrote home on tissue-thin paper:
"Don't worry, Mom, I'll be all right."

3.

Snug in my fug, I stink of old socks,
cocido, vinegar, soiled underwear,
the gunk in coffee cups. I entertain you
and you and you and I am always alone by noon

with the detritus of others: plane ticket stubs,
dental floss, a bent book, a used Q-tip
flecked with a dab of black earwax.
I walk my perrito down Calle Mejía Lequerica.

I pass a young woman with tumors
on her face, hard and green as olives,
her skin gives off a golden Goya glow.
She always wears new bandages

and tries to cover her surgeries with hair.
Her truth stops me every single time.
Estos días azules y este sol de la infancia . . .
is the poem they found in Machado's pocket

when he died, along with a bit of *Hamlet*.
Blue days, I adjust my cashmere scarves,

one mustard colored, one a bicycle design.
It's either cold or hot here like the people.

Madrileños have a saying: Nueve meses
de invierno, tres meses de infierno.
Spain, old gimpy creature, you jump.
Your rump red with pimples. You stomp.

4.

Salvi Melguizo, I am to Spain as the poor
are to the rich, so I am often alone,
which causes time to be mine.
In Gijón I have mildewed walls

the color of teeth stained by espressos.
In my late fifties I sleep with my stench.
In the morning I stand, or lean rather,
into the little balcony, one foot deep

caked thick with pigeon caca,
insect frass, and cigarette butts in a jug.
Along the promenade they air the elderly,
stroll them past the porn shop.

My French bulldog pup wee-wees—
at least I think he's a French bulldog,
that's what I was told, and yet . . .
he's perhaps an accidental bulldog.

It is an extravagance to be perfumed
with his mammal dander as I stand

before the languor of the Spaniards.
All I can say is it took forever to say

what it was I was until I stood in a place
where there was no need to say anything.
Machado, Machado, you gave me a manual
to be my own animal of meaning.

5.

Machado, Machado, Machado!
Slick oiled hair and green Berber coat—
you are my brave love-thug! *I want—*
my heart wants—more light, please,

more life—just one more miracle of spring.
I want what Machado wants. I want . . .
Spain, your thick red shoes scuffed.
Your lips swell with herpes blisters.

Ilk of smacks and thrusts, Spain's a push
a slurp a jib a jig a wag a whip a wiggle
a whack a suck and enough is never enough.
I enter a crowd of capes and lipsticks.

I walk the dog down Gran Vía to Callao.
The dog is neither one breed nor
another and all anyone says is:
"What kind of dog is that?"

Give someone your hand, Spaniards say,
and they'll take your arm.

Here's a plate of olives and some fabada.
Belch, fat little expats, belch!

The food is black and yellow and red.
The dog is named Coco or Coco Loco.
Coco was our priest Franco shot dead.
Hot, formal, my Machado, my Spain.

AT THE PITT RIVERS MUSEUM

Past lawns
at Keble
you coaxed
us the way
apostles do
to pursue you
into corridors
of fossils
peekaboo
kangaroo
General Pitt-Rivers
stuffed stuff
in his hold
or jalopy
and brought
his booty
back to Oxford
gitchy-goo
British boy
ungraspable
elastic goose
four years old
full of wishes

boo-boos
and no-no's
you love to be
naked in public
every skeleton
a cage every
heart a zoo
the last feeble
dodo died
in Mauritius
toodeloo

SIESTA

People not mine
what is it we can hear
the old custodian
coddles the tin box
in the empty church
the ex-monk clips
his lime tree just so
my soiled skin flensed
from my uniform
Jesus said to them
O ye of little faith
Ayamonte is golden
the sun rakes over us
meticulous and slow
a mutt with cataracts
licks its parts ticking
Portugal lies exposed
on her soft cheap cot
passive docile blue
next to my proud Spain
the bull of Europe
the sea's lips shoo me
into my Iberian delirium
gentle and yet firm
nothing here is mine

STILLE NACHT

We met—We loved.
—John Clare

Moon
your nipple
hardens
over

Vienna
we've almost
forgotten
the war

the cuckoo
clock
jabs
a muscle

of music
Hamlet
dismantling
his anguish

the church
chews
Jesus
the Danube

slaps
the buttocks
of Europe
a rabbi

rounds
the rim
stars
zero in

the glitz
of my window
Lo
a man

spits
on a man
splits
him

open
like a Bible

sex
is

an ax

POETA EN NUEVA YORK

FOR ELIZABETH MOE

Nadie es profeta en su tierra.
    —San Lucas 4:24

¿Viste la grieta azul de la luna rota?

Lorca, 5:00 a.m. and I am slathered in Spain:
cologne, exhaust, coffee, chorizo, the tang
of an old body that needs to be washed.
I'm on the top floor. 18 West Tenth Street.
The Emma Lazarus house: "Send these,
the homeless, tempest-tost to me,
I lift my lamp beside the golden door!"
I hold my passport, covered in stamps.
I've double-checked it twice. The moon
in the window is crinkled up like Kleenex.
Now more light—light, here and here,
then there and there—light, light, light,
light—on the Regency desk a framed photo
of Andrew and John, married at Althorpe.
Lorca, two men I love who love each other—
what a privilege to witness a spoken love!

My suitcase open on the floor, wishes packed
like in the Declaration of Independence.
The doctors urged me to come: a stroke,
a brain bleed, my mother's occipital lobe.

Una de las dos Españas ha de helarte el corazón

    Lorca, the sun kisses the city like a Spaniard.
Kiss kiss! I see Wall Street over the balustrade,
where once there were two towers, now
one—everything eventually subtracts.
Frank Doyle, my classmate, died in that.
Frank knew what I now know, when you
become a ghost in one world you become
a guest in another. Leaves fall outside.
Lorca, I am not ready to speak English—
chopped syllables, the tongue less languid.
My mind still preoccupied with the tempo
of Spain, not ready to change languages
like clothes. Spain has no Puritanical itches.
Lorca, on the gay nude beach in Sitges
the empty church stuck out from the shore
like a giant body part. I laid my body down
with the rest and felt free as the sea crashed
against us. I work in a conservative church
in the gay district, the church loves me,
the district loves me, the two do not meet,
always I must deliberate over which is which.

Lorca eran todos

Lorca, what time, what time is it?
My mother's brain bleeds. Once we mounted
a festival in Madrid, and you were there.
Your niece helped me; her eyes so brown
they were black. Showed me your single bed,
how your body had molded the mattress.
The body. And the absence of the body.
All my life my mother and I asked what
countries ask: If we share everything, who are we?
Lorca, when young, in hullabaloo boots, her body
shook and was bound tight as upholstery.
In a moment of bashful pride, my mother said to me:
"I was very well-proportioned, darling."
Doña Maria Teresa back in Madrid, a loyal member,
a former acrobat with tattoos, one misspelled
in English which I don't have the heart to correct,
dresses her Chihuahua in Elton John outfits,
places the semi-blind creature in a bassinet.
She needs paste for her dentures. I proceed
there before Grand Central to buy her Fixodent.
About love I will no longer be frugal.

Dos tiros a García Lorca en el culo, por maricón

Lorca, Santiago to Madrid we traveled—
five hours the Bishop and I sang flamenco,
passing pink isolated brothels where women
lay on mattresses chewing churros, waiting.
Our branch of the church did not approve
of marrying the gays, which made me uneasy.
He attributed my dismay to being American.
America, my country of blabbermouths
and bleached teeth, people who slap their knees.
Nothing I could say to undo his choice.
Or so it seemed. How long could I abide?
Splat went the bugs as they caked the windshield.
I loved the Bishop, which meant I loved him,
Lorca, no matter what he would decide.
"Who is your favorite poet?" I asked.
He was a gato, fifth-generation Madrid.
He paused as more bugs splattered before us
and screamed: "Lorca!" I asked him why.
"He's so sencillo!"—by which he meant, "clear."
Lorca, your poems are the color of stars.

Y echándolo fuera de la ciudad, le apedrearon

    Lorca, bullet holes in the wall in Granada,
some at eye level, others came up to my waist,
where they had knelt, that Goddamned civil war,
all the bodies without names. Christ, Spain—
squat, brown, glabrous, wide as you are tall,
rich as you are small—what happens to us now
that I no longer sit in your love seat of a lap?
Nurses come. Doctors come. Knock, knock.
Lorca, it must be three in the afternoon.
The collected letters of Thom Gunn on my lap.
"Are you the son? The priest? From Spain?"
When you are a foreigner, your heart grows
restrained and restraint becomes who you are.
Connecticut tints the hall battleship gray
in the New London neuroscience wing.
My dear mother, you drool and have become
someone else, you look back, grow salty,
have lost language like luggage. My old love,
my love who gave me language that I love,
when there are no words, there are only acts.

HUMPTY DUMPTY

FOR MARK WUNDERLICH

Iowa
in my
owl-eye
I crack

delicate
Acropolis
Io
fleeing

Wisconsin
Fabergé
Easter
ego

egg
off
the Empire
State

I go I
wow

my hoi polloi
my yolk

my holy
water
Puck
in an ascot

a girlie
Houdini
hemicorporectomy
a jazzy

Capote
swirl
O
Iago

I am
the town
of Santiago
a Stonewall

disco ball
a poof
of Ruth
with Boaz

Christ's
lollipop
an Appomattox
of polka dots

after
the war
Picasso
never went

back
to Spain
Spain
made

his heart
a suitcase

OLD LYME RHYME

I lift up my eyes
in the Big Y aisle
where is my help
where is my help

in the checkout
with our coupons
my father rants
about Republicans

my mother's teeth
the color of worms
her greasy hair
in a topknot

it's a small rental
her secondhand
wheelchair smells
like a compost heap

we eat meals
delivered in black
plastic the sea says
don't think twice

or does it say *you*
cannot do this twice
the cranberry light
dices Connecticut

tints the blue berms
a buoy bell chimes
St. Ann's steeple
splices a sky the color

of a crawl space
my mother urinates
into a commode
on Mile Creek Road

the liquid drums down
on the plastic bucket
like a rain squall
the bureaucrat says

they're on the list
to be dissected
for free and could
we press three

for Social Security
if we wanted a box
in wood or plastic
the prices varied

saltbox houses locked
tight Yankee thrift
where the librarian
smells like mothballs

on Lyme Street
and says *Oh that's nice*
the estuary shifts
with awls and titmice

switchgrass sea myrtle
marsh elder glasswort
sweet pepper bush
austere Connecticut

my mysterious state
remote elegant
next-door lesbians
my mother said

were not lesbians
were swept into urns
Audrey and Bee
Audrey and Bee

EPHPHATHA

FOR DOROTHY MORAN

When the pandemic hit, the priest
died first. Refrigerator trucks chilled the dead.
The parish stacked the hymnals in tubs
and St. Mark's / San Marcos closed in Queens,
the mocked Simon and Garfunkel borough
where coins in dryers clickety-clicked like clocks
in European town squares.

Seven months later, Roosevelt Avenue
jounces with mango slices in ziplocks.
The vestry interviews me. Last day of August,
no AC, we sweat and fidget with our N95 masks.
The wardens, Henry and Jorge, jigger
the broken tumbler to unlock the safe.
"Cut the parish hall in half, don't fundraise,
leverage the lot. Less people in church,"
says a new bishop from his Zoom-perch.

A woman stands in the garden.
Forever a woman stands in the garden.
She rides the 7 to work, is over ninety,

first woman to work on Wall Street.
Much she won't tell or will only tell me.
My invisible incomprehensible work.
I go where I am sent.

A bloated deacon gossips and picks
at the many pimples on his forehead.
O buckling blue esotery falling all apart!
My anonymity increases with each entrance.
Will our hope be transfigured by this dust?
My black uniform sticks to my pocked back
like a sealed envelope.

LITTLE COMPTON PSALM

Universe,
our enemies
delay.
Selah!
Narragansetts
haunt
the circumference.
Wee
village green,
milky
light,
shingled
church.
Christ,
cantilevered
homunculus—
dolorous
as Prokofiev,
I admire
your talent
for stamina.
Whatever
the crisis

the answer
is love.
Where is
my home?
Vagabond,
I drip
with Easter.
How free
these New World
warblers
in the cherry
tree—
their opera
of transience.

VENI CREATOR SPIRITUS

Shakespeare,
Jesus Christ
has a wallet,
a corsage,
nail clippers,
toe jam,
and armpits
like onions.
Seminary
forgot to
tell us.
O bookshelf—
where is
Steven Hobbs?
Forty-one.
Bile duct
cancer. Died
last week.
He published
one short story.

HOSPICE ALTARPIECE

. . . we should be careful

Of each other, we should be kind
While there is still time.
                    —Philip Larkin

1.

Here's to the dinky threshold
where our mother's cocktail dresses molt!
Here's to her crockery found and reglued!
The stinky room bleached by my brother.
We are two bachelors with antibacterial wipes.
Photographs adhere to her diary like shale.
Outside the semidetached rental,
Connecticut nurses her dead ends.
Beyond the sliding glass door,
I plant a pine seedling from Stop & Shop:
my husbandry. I spread the tarot deck—
I draw the Hanged Man, the Death card,
and the Empress upside down.

On the metal morgue table
Sylvia Plath's shoulders bruised blue.

Thrashing in the kitchen before she died,
as if she did not want to be dead.

Truly I tell you, when young,
our mother dillydallied in Pucci and heels.
When old, Mom said, "No pictures."
At the end, she stuck out her hands, a supplicant.
Stella and Linda and Wendy dressed her,
wiped and lathered under her breasts, held Mom,
led her out where she did not want to go.

2.

Theophilus, Theophilus, I speak of love.
What love is, is the story of disciples,
we who fall asleep in the garden.
Always a sacrifice made by someone.
Dad stood before the morgue table
with the curved silver lip, hose, stopper,
drain, pivot rod, clog, trap, and vent
to take the dead apart, while she
raised the boys who would never marry.
Verily, verily, the aide pencils in
an eyebrow on her forehead.

Jean Stein jumped from the balcony.
The same one as Gloria Vanderbilt's son.
Her dress whipped around her like a kite.
What was she thinking as she plummeted?
The family had asked the super to screw
the French doors shut, but . . .

Our father's heart slows. On the toilet
he bleeds out as Charisma wipes his behind.

Says he has failed, lost his money, gave in
to his wife, "She was stupid about money."
But what does it matter in the afterlife?
My brother, once our two danced the jitterbug!
"That's right, I was faithful, never went
with another woman. Sixty years . . ."

3.

    Bless the mechanical hospital bed—
split side rails, controls, casters, alarms—
the room sours with the scent of used diapers.
Bless the tarnished spoon she clinks
against the china bowl from Walmart—
a cowbell in the pasture. Bless the aide
Desiree who rinses out the shit-bucket.
Bless our father nodding off on his watch.
"The photographs," Mom says. "Where are they?"
O Zion, she loved apples—Fuji, Golden Delish.
Praised sentences by Hemingway.
She was a sexy tomboy.

    A friend took his life out in California
where the mangoes and strawberries grow.
I hadn't heard from him in years, a dancer,
a beautiful man named Conor McTeague,
married to a beautiful man. Did it with duct tape
and the exhaust pipe in a car in the desert.
Beautiful men, beautiful men, where will it end?

"Do you get an erection anymore?"
Mom asks. Adjua brushes Dad's gums.
"Not in about ten years," he says, wistful.
"But I have dreams. I have dreams."

BENEDICTUS

Half-assed
Samaritan
on your Camino
de Santiago
conductor

without
an orchestra
black slacks
flocked
with wax

issuing ash
Madame
Bovary
with a rosary
arise marry

Queens
stacked
with axed
Christmas
trees

Pharisees
mocked
childless
Jesus
to pieces

voodoo
doll call
screw your
stepmom
Lady Macbeth

courage
the red
door locked
the parish
not endowed

wafers stale
in an oxidized
ciborium
inky crow
in the barn

tick tock
tick tock
time
to burn
your parents

WYOMING

I put away the burse
the Snake River preaches
her sermon my hearse

it's plain where we go
when we're done cowboy
Sundays we proceed

from the father and the son
something to rehearse
it's a week since Prospero

died at the end I shushed
Dad who looked but could
not see tossed with regret

wanted to be a writer
but instead became
my dictionary of love

once upon a time a father
loved his son a son
loved his father no love

was longer and that's why
I've done what I've done

GLADEVIEW JEU

Once four,
now three!
We her retinue—
Queen of Hearts,

where is
your beau?
Pretty once,
with an opal brooch.

Connecticut,
have you seen
her beau?
O Ophelia,

how's your tummy?
London Bridge
falling down!
Baby Mama—

our aide
from Ghana—
have you seen
his boutonniere?

Loretta,
prettiest name
I know.
We're private,

Spencer,
private
as Hepburn
at Fenwick.

Close the door.
The window
an ambulance
of autumn

we can't open
in our hibernaculum—
orange
October—

gaga
with gutters
and chrysanthemums.
Endymion,

our old moon
wants
red boots!
Where are

her red boots?
Will it snow?
Social worker,
where will

she go?
Once four.
Now three.
A small run.

Gin rummy!
I'm out—
O Queen of Hearts,
Queen of Hearts,

Queen of Hearts,
Queen of Hearts,
where is
your beau?

NUNC DIMITTIS

A mother's universe
is love in reverse.

PILGRIM

Translation of Luis Cernuda

Return? Return? A weak man,
after long years, after a long trip,
worn out from the road, craving
his country, his home, his friends,
a safe kind of love, that man *will* return.

But you? Return? Go back? No,
do not think of it, keep moving forward,
stay alert whether you're a kid or old,
you're not Ulysses, no one looks for you,
there's no Ithaca and no Penelope.

So go on, go on, do *not* go back,
be faithful until the end,
do not wish for any easier destiny,
your feet will track the unknown,
and what's ahead you can never see.

MARÍA MAGDALENA

FOR LAURA GARCÍA-LORCA DE LOS RÍOS

I kept vigil. Preferred shadows.
When I spoke, a man interrupted me.
Someone called me a bitch. *The bird*
on the branch then suddenly, it's gone.
I forgot your name. Yelled from a ditch.
You've no idea what it was like.
Occupied my sex, barely, but—

Remember the rain?
The tree in silence, but suddenly,
the wind. Some talked about the past.
Whatever was the point of it all?
I held on through such argument!
Wished I winced less, but—
I was alone. The moon fondled me.
Was *thrilled* to be fondled. I ached
in the arches of my feet. I was wrong—
about much.
                    Believing I was alone . . .
I lingered, planted a garden,
hammered in stakes with names.

We waited. God, did we wait.
I washed cutlery to make a music.
Complicated the horizon like a lilac.
No one noticed me. Not really.
Which was a relief.

    A bird in the wind—
brings the memory of you back.
Suddenly I see with the light of your eyes.
My country? Did I have a country?
¿Mi país? ¿Tuve un país?
Stupid to bank on belonging,
I always knew that. I belonged to the Lord.
People laughed when I said that.
I no longer cared.

    When my nailed human was free,
                      I left.

NOTE

"San Sebastián" italicizes lines I translated from Federico García Lorca's play *Amor de Don Perlimplín con Belisa en su jardín.* "María Magdalena" italicizes lines I translated from Francisco García Lorca's poem "De pronto."

ACKNOWLEDGMENTS

The Adroit Journal
The American Poetry Review
Anglican Theological Review
The Cortland Review
EcoTheo Review

Letters from Spain
HBP, Inc.
Kirby Family Foundation

The FSG Poetry Anthology
The Paris Review
Poem-a-Day
Poetry
Poetry Daily
Queensbound
Queer Poem-a-Day
Rhino
Upstreet

Red Door Series
St. John's Episcopal Church
Jackson Hole, Wyoming

Desperate Literature
Unamuno Author Festival
Desperate Literature, Residencia de
Estudiantes, el Instante Fundación
Madrid, Spain

Diván
Centro and Fundación Federico García Lorca
Granada, Spain

Yaddo

Civitella Ranieri